# THE SCHOOL SHOOTER: A THREAT ASSESSMENT PERSPECTIVE

**Mary Ellen O'Toole, PhD**
**Supervisory Special Agent**
**Federal Bureau of Investigation**

Youth violence has been one of the greatest single crime problems we face in this country. We have focused on this problem, working in partnership with state and local governments to develop prevention and enforcement programs that work. Youth who commit crimes of violence must be held accountable, and the punishment must be firm and fair and fit the crime. At the same time, we must do everything we can to prevent crime in the first place.

We have shown that if communities, schools, government and other key players pull together to address the roots of violence, we can make America safer for our children. Communities around the country are proving that prevention and intervention strategies that help keep our young people out of trouble do work. It is, therefore, critical that we do all we can to identify young people who need our help, and then get them the help they need.

We must continue to search for those crucial behavioral and environmental indicators which suggest that a threat of school violence may be real. That is why this report, "The School Shooter: A Threat Assessment Perspective," is so important. Although much research remains to be done, this report serves as a vital foundation. It presents a model procedure for threat assessment and intervention--including a chapter on key indicators that should be regarded as warning signs in evaluating threats.

If we use this threat assessment model judiciously--and we must, because the risk of unfairly labeling and stigmatizing children is great--then we will be able to fight, and win, the war on two fronts. We will be in a position to help those children who show a propensity for violence, before they scar themselves (and others) forever. And we will be in a position to protect innocent school children before they become senseless victims.

Janet Reno

**U.S. Department of Justice**

Federal Bureau of Investigation

---

Office of the Director

*Washington, D.C. 20535*

## MESSAGE FROM FBI DIRECTOR FREEH

I know I speak for every parent and every educator in the nation when I say that violence in our schools is not acceptable, not at all, not ever. It is imperative that, community by community, we find the ways to protect our children and secure for them the safe places they need to learn the hard business of growing up, to learn right from wrong, to learn to be good citizens.

I am, therefore, deeply appreciative of the unprecedented effort by experts from so many different disciplines that produced this practical resource, *The School Shooter: A Threat Assessment* Perspective. It is aimed at prevention: identifying the precursors of violence through threat assessments, then initiating an intervention process to stop violent acts before they erupt. I would like to thank all who participated in the study and to pledge the FBI's resources, support, and assistance in this cause of prevention. We want to work with America's schools now, not when they have tragically become a crime scene.

Above all, I would like to dedicate this resource to the educators and parents who will use it--you who care so much and try so hard to create safe places of learning. Thank you for your efforts. Thank you for taking responsibility to protect our most precious resource--our children.

Louis J. Freeh

# TABLE OF CONTENTS

# CHAPTER I

## INTRODUCTION

Why would a student bring a weapon to school and without any explicable reason open fire on fellow students and teachers? Are school shooters angry? Are they crazy? Is their motive revenge? Hatred for the victims? A hunger for attention?

The origins of human violence are complex. Thinkers, historians, and scientists have explored the issue for centuries, but answers remain elusive. The roots of a violent act are multiple, intricate, and intertwined. The mix of factors varies according to the individual and the circumstances. Understanding violence after it has occurred is difficult enough. Trying to assess a threat and keep it from being carried out is even more of a challenge.

This monograph presents a systematic procedure for threat assessment and intervention. The model is designed to be used by educators, mental health professionals and law enforcement agencies. Obviously, the same events that led the National Center for the Analysis of Violent Crime (NCAVC) to this subject have also led school administrators and law enforcement officials across the country to consider and develop their own policies and procedures for dealing with threats or acts of violence in schools. This model is offered in the hope that it may help refine and strengthen those efforts. Its fundamental building blocks are the threat assessment standards outlined in Chapter II, which provide a framework for evaluating a spoken, written, and symbolic threat, and the four-pronged assessment approach, which will be described in Chapter III and provides a logical, methodical process to examine the threatener and assess the risk that the threat will be carried out.

***This model is not a "profile" of the school shooter or a checklist of danger signs pointing to the next adolescent who will bring lethal violence to a school. Those things do not exist. Although the risk of an actual shooting incident in any one school is very low, threats of violence are potentially a problem in any school. Once a threat is made, having a fair, rational, and standardized method of evaluating and responding to threats is critically important.***

### NCAVC's Study and the Leesburg Symposium

The monograph was developed from the concepts and principles developed by the FBI's NCAVC in nearly 25 years of experience in threat assessment, ideas generated at a 1999 NCAVC symposium on school shootings, and an in-depth review of eighteen school shooting cases.

In May, 1998, the NCAVC initiated a research initiative to study the recent occurrences of school shootings, from a behavioral perspective. The original research was designed to study specific cases of school shootings or foiled attempts in order to develop a better understanding of these events -- the incident itself, and the shooter, his background, the school, and other social dynamics which may have influenced the crime. Eighteen cases were ultimately identified and included in the study. (These cases are not identified in this monograph because of confidentiality issues.)

The shooting at Columbine High School in Littleton, Colorado, in April 1999, shocked the country and gave new urgency to the FBI's research effort. With the support of Attorney General Janet M. Reno and FBI Director Louis J. Freeh, the FBI's NCAVC invited 160 educators, administrators, mental health professionals, law enforcement officers, and prosecutors to a symposium on school shootings and threat assessment. The symposium took place in Leesburg, Virginia, in July 1999. In attendance were teachers and administrators from all eighteen schools involved in the NCAVC study (including someone from each school who knew the shooter or would-be shooter personally), NCAVC staff members, and law enforcement officers who were involved in investigating each of the shootings. Also attending were experts in disciplines including adolescent violence, mental health, suicidology, school dynamics, and family dynamics.

### The School Shooter Phenomenon and Threat Assessment

Adolescent violence in general, and homicides in particular, have decreased since 1993, but that hopeful trend has been somewhat obscured in the nationwide wave of concern over school shootings of the type examined in NCAVC's study. This recent form of adolescent violence is in fact quite rare. But the sudden, senseless deaths of teenagers and teachers in the middle of a school day, for no comprehensible reason, is far more shocking and gets far more attention than the less extreme acts of violence that happen in schools every week.

Under the intense spotlight of national media coverage, a tragedy such as the Columbine High School shooting spreads horror, shock, and fear to every corner of the country. Educators, mental health professionals, legislators, law enforcement officers, parents, students, and the rest of the public all share a sense of frustration and helplessness and a compulsion to take some quick action that can prevent similar incidents in the future. Though understandable, this impulse can lead communities to forget the wisdom of H. L. Mencken's aphorism: "For every problem, there is a solution which is simple, neat, and wrong." In a knee-jerk reaction, communities may resort to inflexible, one-size-fits-all policies on preventing or reacting to violence.

One response to the pressure for action may be an effort to identify the next shooter by developing a "profile" of the typical school shooter. This may sound like a reasonable preventive measure, but in practice, trying to draw up a catalogue or "checklist" of warning signs to detect a potential school shooter can be shortsighted, even dangerous. Such lists, publicized by the media, can end up unfairly labeling many nonviolent students as potentially dangerous or even lethal. In fact, a great many adolescents who will never commit violent acts will show some of the behaviors or personality traits included on the list.

In the wake of a school shooting there is often an outcry for immediate response in the form of more stringent security precautions in schools or stricter laws aimed at school violence. However, these demands have been accompanied by little if any concerted and organized effort to understand the roots of school shooting incidents. How did a particular student come to the point of feeling that shooting fellow students and teachers was in some way an answer to his problems or emotional needs? Were there signs along the way -- not a catalogue of traits identifying him as a predicted killer, but clues that could have indicated a need for help? What was the influence of family, friends, and community?

The issue facing educators, law enforcement agencies, and the wider public is not how to predict school violence. Reliably predicting any type of violence is extremely difficult. Predicting that an individual who has never acted out violently in the past will do so in the future is still more difficult. Seeking to predict acts that occur as rarely as school shootings is almost impossible. This is simple statistical logic: when the incidence of any form of violence is very low and a very large number of people have identifiable risk factors, there is no reliable way to pick out from that large group the very few who will actually commit the violent act.

After a violent incident has taken place, retracing an offender's past and identifying clues that in retrospect could have been signs of danger can yield significant, useful information. However, even clues that appear to help interpret past events should not be taken as predictors of similar events in the future. At this time, there is no research that has identified traits and characteristics that can reliably distinguish school shooters from other students. Many students appear to have traits and characteristics similar to those observed in students who were involved in school shootings.

### *Misinformation About School Shootings*

Though school shootings are extensively covered in the news media, the information available in news reports is not necessarily complete, accurate, or balanced. News coverage is inherently hasty and often relies on sources who themselves have incomplete or inaccurate information. And journalists ordinarily do not have access to police and other investigative reports that may contain highly significant but confidential information about a school shooting incident or about the background, previous activities, and traits of the student or students who carried out the shooting.

To the extent that academics, researchers, and other specialists writing in professional publications base their articles on news accounts or other public sources, these too should be viewed with some reservations since they will also lack critical information available only in confidential school or law enforcement files.

News coverage magnifies a number of widespread but wrong or unverified impressions of school shooters. Among them are:

- School violence is an epidemic.

- All school shooters are alike.

- The school shooter is always a loner.

- School shootings are exclusively revenge motivated.

- Easy access to weapons is THE most significant risk factor.

Unusual or aberrant behaviors, interests, hobbies, etc., are hallmarks of the student destined to become violent.

**School shootings and other forms of school violence are not just a school's problem or a law enforcement problem. They involve schools, families, and the communities. An adolescent comes to school with a collective life experience, both positive and negative, shaped by the environments of family, school, peers, community, and culture. Out of that collective experience come values, prejudices, biases, emotions, and the student's responses to training, stress, and authority. His or her behavior at school is affected by the entire range of experiences and influences. No one factor is decisive. By the same token, however, no one factor is completely without effect, which means that when a student has shown signs of potential violent behavior, schools and other community institutions do have the capacity -- and the responsibility -- to keep that potential from turning real.\***

---

\*The threats which some schools face may not fall within the experience of the NCAVC. For example, some urban schools have experienced threats not like the threats represented in this monograph. Therefore, the applicability of the recommendations made in this monograph may not cover all situations.

# CHAPTER II

## *ASSESSING THREATS*

*All threats are NOT created equal*. However, all threats should be accessed in a timely manner and decisions regarding how they are handled must be done quickly.

In today's climate, some schools tend to adopt a one-size-fits-all approach to any mention of violence. The response to every threat is the same, regardless of its credibility or the likelihood that it will be carried out. In the shock-wave of recent school shootings, this reaction may be understandable, but it is exaggerated -- and perhaps dangerous, leading to potential underestimation of serious threats, overreaction to less serious ones, and unfairly punishing or stigmatizing students who are in fact not dangerous. A school that treats all threats as equal falls into the fallacy formulated by Abraham Maslow: "If the only tool you have is a hammer, you tend to see every problem as a nail." Every problem is not a nail, of course, and schools must recognize that every threat does not represent the same danger or require the same level of response.

Some threats can herald a clear and present danger of a tragedy on the scale of Columbine High School. Others represent little or no real threat to anyone's safety. Neither should be ignored, but reacting to both in the same manner is ineffective and self-defeating. In every school, an established threat assessment procedure managed by properly trained staff can help school administrators and other school staff distinguish between different levels of threats and choose different appropriate responses.

Threat assessment seeks to make an informed judgment on two questions: how credible and serious is the threat itself? And to what extent does the threatener appear to have the resources, intent, and motivation to carry out the threat?

**A systematic approach to threat assessment should be part of the nationwide approach advocated by Attorney General Janet Reno and Secretary of Education Richard W. Riley in a 1998 letter to principals and teachers, calling for "an overall effort to make sure that every school in the Nation has a comprehensive violence prevention plan in place." Their letter, which introduced the joint Justice and Education Department publication "Early Warning, Timely Response: A Guide to Safe Schools," added this cautionary advice: "We also caution you to recognize that over labeling and using this guide to stigmatize children in a cursory way that leads to overreaction is harmful."**

The NCAVC threat assessment-intervention model presented in this paper can be used by educators, law enforcement officers, mental health professionals, and others involved in school safety. It outlines a methodical procedure for evaluating a threat and the person making the threat, with the aim of reaching an informed judgment on the danger that a violent act will actually be carried out. To use the model effectively, those making the assessments should have appropriate training.

### *What is a Threat?*

A threat is an expression of intent to do harm or act out violently against someone or something. A threat can be spoken, written, or symbolic -- for example, motioning with one's hands as though shooting at another person.

Threat assessment rests on two critical principles: first, that all threats and all threateners are not equal; second, that most threateners are unlikely to carry out their threat. However, all threats must be taken seriously and evaluated.

In NCAVC's experience, most threats are made anonymously or under a false name. Because threat assessment relies heavily on evaluating the threatener's background, personality, lifestyle, and resources, identifying the threatener is necessary for an informed assessment to be made -- and also so criminal charges can be brought if the threat is serious enough to warrant prosecution. If the threatener's identity cannot be determined, the response will have to be based on an assessment of the threat alone. That assessment may change if the threatener is eventually identified: a threat that was considered low risk may be rated as more serious if new information suggests the threatener is dangerous, or conversely, an assessment of high risk may be scaled down if the threatener is identified and found not to have the intent, ability, means, or motive to carry out the threat.

### *Motivation*

Threats are made for a variety of reasons. A threat may be a warning signal, a reaction to fear of punishment or some other anxiety, or a demand for attention. It may be intended to taunt; to intimidate; to assert power or control; to punish; to manipulate or coerce; to frighten; to terrorize; to compel someone to do something; to strike back for an injury, injustice or slight; to disrupt someone's or some institution's life; to test authority, or to protect oneself. The emotions that underlie a threat can be love; hate; fear; rage; or desire for attention, revenge, excitement, or recognition.

Motivation can never be known with complete certainty, but to the extent possible, understanding motive is a key element in evaluating a threat. A threat will reflect the threatener's mental and emotional state at the time the threat was made, but it is important to remember that a state of mind can be temporarily but strongly influenced by alcohol or drugs, or a precipitating incident such as a romantic breakup, failing grades, or conflict with a parent. After a person has absorbed an emotional setback and calmed down, or when the effects of alcohol or drugs have worn off, his motivation to act on a violent threat may also have diminished.

*Signposts*

In general, people do not switch instantly from nonviolence to violence. Nonviolent people do not "snap" or decide on the spur of the moment to meet a problem by using violence. Instead, the path toward violence is an evolutionary one, with signposts along the way. A threat is one observable behavior; others may be brooding about frustration or disappointment, fantasies of destruction or revenge, in conversations, writings, drawings, and other actions.

*Types of Threats*

Threats can be classed in four categories: *direct, indirect, veiled,* or *conditional.*

*A direct threat* identifies a specific act against a specific target and is delivered in a straightforward, clear, and explicit manner: "I am going to place a bomb in the school's gym."

*An indirect threat* tends to be vague, unclear, and ambiguous. The plan, the intended victim, the motivation, and other aspects of the threat are masked or equivocal: "If I wanted to, I could kill everyone at this school!" While violence is implied, the threat is phrased tentatively -- "If I wanted to" -- and suggests that a violent act COULD occur, not that it WILL occur.

*A veiled threat* is one that strongly implies but does not explicitly threaten violence. "We would be better off without you around anymore" clearly hints at a possible violent act, but leaves it to the potential victim to interpret the message and give a definite meaning to the threat.

*A conditional threat* is the type of threat often seen in extortion cases. It warns that a violent act will happen unless certain demands or terms are met: "If you don't pay me one million dollars, I will place a bomb in the school."

*Factors in Threat Assessment*

*Specific, plausible details* are a critical factor in evaluating a threat. Details can include the identity of the victim or victims; the reason for making the threat; the means, weapon, and method by which it is to be carried out; the date, time, and place where the threatened act will occur; and concrete information about plans or preparations that have already been made.

Specific details can indicate that substantial thought, planning, and preparatory steps have already been taken, suggesting a higher risk that the threatener will follow through on his threat. Similarly, a lack of detail suggests the threatener may not have thought through all of the contingencies, has not actually taken steps to carry out the threat, and may not seriously intend violence but is "blowing off steam" over some frustration or seeking to frighten or intimidate a particular victim or disrupt a school's events or routine.

Details that are specific but not logical or plausible may indicate a less serious threat. For example, a high school student writes that he intends to detonate hundreds of pounds of plutonium in the school's auditorium the following day at lunch time. The threat is detailed, stating a specific time, place, and weapon. But the details are unpersuasive. Plutonium is almost impossible to obtain, legally or on the black market. It is expensive, hard to transport, and very dangerous to handle, and a complex high explosive detonation is required to set off a nuclear reaction. No high school student is likely to have any plutonium at all, much less hundreds of pounds, nor would he have the knowledge or complex equipment to detonate it. A threat this unrealistic is obviously unlikely to be carried out.

*The emotional content of a threat* can be an important clue to the threatener's mental state. Emotions are conveyed by melodramatic words and unusual punctuation -- "I hate you!!!!!" "You have ruined my life!!!!" "May God have mercy on your soul!!!!" -- or in excited, incoherent passages that may refer to God or other religious beings or deliver an ultimatum.

Though emotionally charged threats can tell the assessor something about the temperament of the threatener, they are not a measure of danger. They may sound frightening, but no correlation has been established between the emotional intensity in a threat and the risk that it will be carried out.

*Precipitating stressors* are incidents, circumstances, reactions, or situations which can trigger a threat. The precipitating event may seem insignificant and have no direct relevance to the threat, but nonetheless becomes a catalyst. For example, a student has a fight with his mother before going to school. The argument may have been a minor one over an issue that had nothing to do with school, but it sets off an emotional chain reaction leading the student to threaten another student at school that day -- possibly something he has thought about in the past.

The impact of a precipitating event will obviously depend on *"pre-disposing factors"*: underlying personality traits, characteristics, and temperament that predispose an adolescent to fantasize about violence or act violently. Accordingly, information about a temporary "trigger" must be considered together with broader information about these underlying factors, such as a student's vulnerability to loss and depression.

## *Levels of Risk*

*Low Level of Threat*: A threat which poses a minimal risk to the victim and public safety.

★ Threat is vague and indirect.
★ Information contained within the threat is inconsistent, implausible or lacks detail.

★ Threat lacks realism.
★ Content of the threat suggests person is unlikely to carry it out.

***Medium Level of Threat***: A threat which could be carried out, although it may not appear entirely realistic.

★ Threat is more direct and more concrete than a low level threat.
★ Wording in the threat suggests that the threatener has given some thought to how the act will be carried out.
★ There may be a general indication of a possible place and time (though these signs still fall well short of a detailed plan).
★ There is no strong indication that the threatener has taken preparatory steps, although there may be some veiled reference or ambiguous or inconclusive evidence pointing to that possibility -- an allusion to a book or movie that shows the planning of a violent act, or a vague, general statement about the availability of weapons.
★ There may be a specific statement seeking to convey that the threat is not empty: "I'm serious!" or "I really mean this!"

***High Level of Threat***: A threat that appears to pose an imminent and serious danger to the safety of others.

★ Threat is direct, specific and plausible.
★ Threat suggests concrete steps have been taken toward carrying it out, for example, statements indicating that the threatener has acquired or practiced with a weapon or has had the victim under surveillance.

**Example:** *"At eight o'clock tomorrow morning, I intend to shoot the principal. That's when he is in the office by himself. I have a 9mm. Believe me, I know what I am doing. I am sick and tired of the way he runs this school."* This threat is direct, specific as to the victim, motivation, weapon, place, and time, and indicates that the threatener knows his target's schedule and has made preparations to act on the threat.

*NCAVC's experience in analyzing a wide range of threatening communications suggests that in general, the more direct and detailed a threat is, the more serious the risk of its being acted on. A threat that is assessed as high level will almost always require immediate law enforcement intervention.*

In some cases, the distinction between the levels of threat may not be as obvious, and there will be overlap between the categories. Generally, obtaining additional information about, either the threat or the threatener will help in clarifying any confusion. What is important is that schools be able to recognize and act on the most serious threats, and then address all other threats appropriately and in a standardized and timely fashion.

# CHAPTER III

## FOUR-PRONGED ASSESSMENT APPROACH

### The Four-Pronged Assessment Model

This innovative model is designed to assess someone who has made a threat and evaluate the likelihood that the threat will actually be carried out.  Anyone can deliver a spoken or written message that sounds foreboding or sinister, but evaluating the threat alone will not establish if the person making it has the intention, the ability, or the means to act on the threat.  To make that determination, assessing the threatener is critical.

Educators, law enforcement, mental health professionals and others must realize they cannot handle threats in the same "old" way.  Those tasked with assessing threats must be trained in the basic concepts of threat assessment, personality assessment and risk assessment as presented in this monograph, and realize the importance of assessing all threats in a timely manner.

What information about students can help us tell which threateners are likely to carry out their threats?  Their age?  Their grades in chemistry class?  Their socioeconomic level?  The experience of the NCAVC is that frequently, only limited information is known about someone being evaluated for threat assessment, or information may be available only in certain areas -- a student's academic record, or family life, or health.  All aspects of a threatener's life must be considered when evaluating whether a threat is likely to be carried out.  This model provides a framework for evaluating a student in order to determine if he or she has the motivation, means, and intent to carry out a proclaimed threat.  The assessment is based on the "totality of the circumstances" known about the student in four major areas:[1]

*Prong One*:   **Personality of the student**

*Prong Two:*   **Family dynamics**

*Prong Three:* **School dynamics and the student's role in those dynamics**

*Prong Four*:   **Social dynamics**

Here is how the Four-Pronged Assessment Model can be used when a threat is received at

---

[1](One of the most important recommendations of this monograph is that additional empirical research be conducted in the area of threat assessment and school violence.  Following this additional research, it may be determined that one or more of the four prongs plays a more significant role than the others in threat assessment.)

a school: A preliminary assessment is done on the threat itself, as outlined in the preceding chapter. If the threatener's identity is known, a threat assessor quickly collects as much information as is available in the four categories. The assessor may be a school psychologist, counselor, or other staff member or specialist who has been designated and trained for this task. Information can come from the assessor's personal knowledge of the student or can be sought from teachers, staff, other students (when appropriate), parents, and other appropriate sources such as law enforcement agencies or mental health specialists.

If the student appears to have serious problems in the majority of the four prongs or areas and if the threat is assessed as high or medium level, the threat should be taken more seriously and appropriate intervention by school authorities and/or law enforcement should be initiated as quickly as possible.

In order to effect a rapid assessment, it may not be possible to evaluate a student thoroughly in each of the four prongs. Nonetheless, having as much information as possible about a student and his or her life is important in order to determine if that student is capable and under enough stressors to carry out a threat.

The following section outlines factors to be considered in each of the four prongs:

### Personality of the Student: Behavior Characteristics and Traits

According to Webster's, personality is "the pattern of collective character, behavioral, temperamental, emotional, and mental traits of an individual." This pattern is a product of both inherited temperament and environmental influences. Personality shapes how people consistently view the world and themselves and how they interact with others. Forming an accurate impression of someone's personality requires observing his or her behavior over a period of time and in a wide variety of situations.

Understanding adolescent personality development is extremely important in assessing any threat made by someone in that age group. An adolescent's personality is not yet crystallized. It is still developing. During adolescence, young people are likely to explore or engage in what others perceive as strange behavior. Adolescents struggle with vulnerability and acceptance ("Am I lovable and able to love?"), with questions of independence and dependence, and with how to deal with authority, among other difficult issues.[2]

---

[2]The 1999 Institutes of Medicine's (IOM) Report on Adolescents, published by the National Science Foundation, states that adolescence is frequently divided into three stages: early (ages 10-14) involving biological puberty, sexual and psychological awakening and self-awareness; middle (ages 15-17) a time of increased autonomy and experimentation and late (ages 18 to early 20's) for those who delay entry into adult independence and autonomy. Each stage produces opportunities, challenges and risks. For example, most (60 percent +) experiment with alcohol and drugs before age 15. Teasing and physical fighting is more frequent at ages 13-14 than at age 16-17. Violent criminal activity generally peaks between the ages

Clues to a student's personality can come from observing behavior when the student is:

- Coping with conflicts, disappointments, failures, insults, or other stresses encountered in everyday life.

- Expressing anger or rage, frustration, disappointment, humiliation, sadness, or similar feelings.

- Demonstrating or failing to demonstrate resiliency after a setback, a failure, real or perceived criticism, disappointment, or other negative experiences.

- Demonstrating how the student feels about himself, what kind of person the student imagines himself or herself to be, and how the student believes he or she appears to others.

- Responding to rules, instruction, or authority figures.

- Demonstrating and expressing a desire or need for control, attention, respect, admiration, confrontation, or other needs.

- Demonstrating or failing to demonstrate empathy with the feelings and experiences of others.

- Demonstrating his or her attitude toward others. (For example, does the student view others as inferior or with disrespect?)

Assessors who have not been able to observe a student first-hand should seek information from those *who knew the student before he or she made a threat.*

### *Family Dynamics*

---

of 15-17. About 25 percent of the adolescent population is at high risk for psycho-social problems and poor developmental outcomes such as academic failure, alcohol and other drug abuse, delinquency and problems with the law and violence. Twenty percent have a diagnosable mental health disorder at sometime during adolescence, the highest rate for any age group through the life-span. Adolescents are more diverse and heterogeneous than originally believed. Important interaction between hormonal, social, and environmental factors shape development and behavior during this period. The IOM reports that the social context in which the adolescent is developing has markedly changed during the past decade - with an increase in many negative factors, including less adult supervision. Adolescence now begins earlier - as early as age nine - and is second only to infancy in growth and change. Their social cognition is different from adults and strongly influences the adolescents' decision-making. They experience emotions more intensely than adults, process information differently, and as a result make decisions differently. These factors are critical for evaluators to be skilled in recognizing the information gathered and observations of youth. It is important to observe and gather information in order to understand the context of adolescent development (K. Dwyer, personal communication, February 2000).

Family dynamics are patterns of behavior, thinking, beliefs, traditions, roles, customs and values that exist in a family. When a student has made a threat, knowledge of the dynamics within the student's family -- and how those dynamics are perceived by both the student and the parents -- is a key factor in understanding circumstances and stresses in the student's life that could play a role in any decision to carry out the threat.

### School Dynamics

The relationship between school dynamics and threat assessment has not been empirically established and therefore its level of significance can either increase or decrease depending on additional research into these cases. *While it may be difficult for educators/assessors to "critique" their own school, it is necessary to have some level of understanding of the particular dynamics in their school because their school can ultimately become the scene of the crime.*

School dynamics are patterns of behavior, thinking, beliefs, customs, traditions, roles and values that exist in a school's culture. Some of these patterns can be obvious, and others subtle. Identifying those behaviors which are formally or informally valued and rewarded in a school helps explain why some students get more approval and attention from school authorities and have more prestige among their fellow students. It can also explain the "role" a particular student is given by the school's culture, and how the student may see himself or herself fitting in, or failing to fit in, with the school's value system.

Students and staff may have very different perceptions of the culture, customs, and values in their school. Assessors need to be aware of how a school's dynamics are seen by students. A big discrepancy between students' perceptions and the administration's can itself be a significant piece of information for the assessor.

### Social Dynamics

Social dynamics are patterns of behavior, thinking, beliefs, customs, traditions, and roles that exist in the larger community where students live. These patterns also have an impact on students' behavior, their feelings about themselves, their outlook on life, attitudes, perceived options, and lifestyle practices. An adolescent's beliefs and opinions, his choices of friends, activities, entertainment, and reading material, and his attitudes toward such things as drugs, alcohol, and weapons will all reflect in some fashion the social dynamics of the community where he lives and goes to school.

Within the larger community, an adolescent's peer group plays an especially crucial role in influencing attitudes and behavior. Information about a student's choice of friends and relations with his peers can provide valuable clues to his attitudes, sense of identity, and possible decisions about acting or not acting on a threat.

# CHAPTER IV

*FINDINGS*

This chapter lists certain types of behavior, personality traits, and circumstances in the family, school, and community environment that should be regarded as warning signs if all or most of them -- in all four categories -- seem to fit a student who has made a threat.

**It should be strongly emphasized that this list is not intended as a checklist to predict future violent behavior by a student who has not acted violently or threatened violence. Rather, the list should be considered only <u>after</u> a student has made some type of threat and an assessment has been developed using the four-pronged model. If the assessment shows evidence of these characteristics, behaviors and consistent problems in all four areas or prongs, it can indicate that the student may be fantasizing about acting on the threat, has the motivation to carry out the violent act, or has actually taken steps to carry out a threat.**

The following cautions should also be emphasized:

1. *No one or two traits or characteristics should be considered in isolation or given more weight than the others.* Any of these traits, or several, can be seen in students who are not contemplating a school shooting or other act of violence. The key to identifying a potentially dangerous threatener under this four-pronged assessment model is that there is evidence of problems on a majority of the items in each of the four areas. **However, there is no "magical" number of traits or constellation of traits which will determine what students may present a problem . Hopefully, subsequent empirical research in this area will determine which are the significant traits and how they should be weighted. However, a practical and common sense application of this model indicates that the more problems which are identified in each of the four prongs, the greater the level of concern for the assessor.**

2. *Behavior is an expression of personality, but one bad day may not reflect a student's real personality or usual behavior pattern.* Accurately evaluating someone's behavior requires establishing a baseline -- how he or she typically behaves most of the time. Those responsible for assessing a student should seek information from people who have known the student over a period of time and have been able to observe him in varying situations and with a variety of people.

3. *Many of the behaviors and traits listed below are seen in depressed adolescents with narcissistic personality characteristics and other possible mental health problems. Despite the overlap between this list and diagnostic symptoms, evaluation under the four-pronged threat assessment model cannot be a substitute for a clinical diagnosis of mental illness.* Signs of serious mental illness and/or substance abuse disorders can significantly elevate the risk for

violence and should be evaluated by a mental health professional.

The following list of behaviors and traits, grouped in the four areas of the assessment model, was developed from three sources: NCAVC's extensive experience in assessing threats for over two decades, including current cases of threats made in schools; ideas presented at the 1999 Leesburg symposium; and NCAVC's intensive review of eighteen school shooting cases.

Subject to the cautionary points mentioned above, the list identifies particular behaviors, personality traits and family, school and social dynamics that may be associated with violence.

### *Prong One: Personality Traits and Behavior*

### ● *Leakage*

"Leakage" occurs when a student intentionally or unintentionally reveals clues to feelings, thoughts, fantasies, attitudes, or intentions that may signal an impending violent act. These clues can take the form of subtle threats, boasts, innuendos, predictions, or ultimatums. They may be spoken or conveyed in stories, diary entries, essays, poems, letters, songs, drawings, doodles, tattoos, or videos.

Another form of leakage involves efforts to get unwitting friends or classmates to help with preparations for a violent act, at times through deception (for example, the student asks a friend to obtain ammunition for him because he is going hunting).

Leakage can be a cry for help, a sign of inner conflict, or boasts that may look empty but actually express a serious threat. Leakage is considered to be one of the most important clues that may precede an adolescent's violent act.

> **An example of leakage could be a student who shows a recurring preoccupation with themes of violence, hopelessness, despair, hatred, isolation, loneliness, nihilism, or an "end-of-the-world" philosophy. Those themes may be expressed in conversation or in jokes or in seemingly offhand comments to friends, teachers, other school employees, parents, or siblings. Statements may be subtle, or immediately minimized by comments such as, "I was just joking," or "I didn't really mean that."**

> **Another example of leakage could be recurrent themes of destruction or violence appearing in a student's writing or artwork. The themes may involve hatred, prejudice, death, dismemberment, mutilation of self or others, bleeding, use of excessively destructive weapons, homicide, or suicide. Many adolescents are fascinated with violence and the macabre, and writings and drawings on these themes can be a reflection of a harmless but rich and**

creative fantasy life. Some adolescents, however, seem so obsessed with these themes that they emerge no matter what the subject matter, the conversation, the assignment, or the joke. In an actual case, a student was taking a home economics class and was assigned to bake something. He baked a cake in the shape of a gun. His school writings and other work also contained recurrent themes of violence.

## ● *Low Tolerance for Frustration*

The student is easily bruised, insulted, angered, and hurt by real or perceived injustices done to him by others and has great difficulty tolerating frustration.

## ● *Poor Coping Skills*

The student consistently shows little if any ability to deal with frustration, criticism, disappointment, failure, rejection, or humiliation. His or her response is typically inappropriate, exaggerated, immature, or disproportionate.

## ● *Lack of Resiliency*

The student lacks resiliency and is unable to bounce back even when some time has elapsed since a frustrating or disappointing experience, a setback, or putdown.

## ● *Failed Love Relationship*

The student may feel rejected or humiliated after the end of a love relationship, and cannot accept or come to terms with the rejection.

## ● *"Injustice Collector"*

The student nurses resentment over real or perceived injustices. No matter how much time has passed, the "injustice collector" will not forget or forgive those wrongs or the people he or she believes are responsible. The student may keep a hit list with the names of people he feels have wronged him.

## ● *Signs of Depression*

The student shows features of depression such as lethargy, physical fatigue, a morose or dark outlook on life, a sense of malaise, and loss of interest in activities that he once enjoyed.

Adolescents may show different signs than those normally associated with depression. Some depressed adolescents may display unpredictable and uncontrolled outbursts of anger, a generalized and excessive hatred toward everyone else, and feelings of hopelessness about the future. Other behaviors might include psychomotor agitation, restlessness, inattention, sleep and eating disorders, and a markedly diminished interest in almost all activities that previously occupied and interested him. The student may have difficulty articulating these extreme feelings.

## ● *Narcissism*

The student is self-centered, lacks insight into others' needs and/or feelings, and blames others for failures and disappointments. The narcissistic student may embrace the role of a victim to elicit sympathy and to feel temporarily superior to others. He or she displays signs of paranoia, and assumes an attitude of self-importance or grandiosity that masks feelings of unworthiness (Malmquist, 1996). A narcissistic student may be either very thin-skinned or very thick-skinned in responding to criticism.

## ● *Alienation*

The student consistently behaves as though he feels different or estranged from others. This sense of separateness is more than just being a loner. It can involve feelings of isolation, sadness, loneliness, not belonging, and not fitting in.

## ● *Dehumanizes Others*

The student consistently fails to see others as fellow humans. He characteristically views other people as "nonpersons" or objects to be thwarted. This attitude may appear in the student's writings and artwork, in interactions with others, or in comments during conversation.

## ● *Lack of Empathy*

The student shows an inability to understand the feelings of others, and appears unconcerned about anyone else's feelings. When others show emotion, the student may ridicule them as weak or stupid.

## ● *Exaggerated Sense of Entitlement*

The student constantly expects special treatment and consideration, and reacts negatively if he doesn't get the treatment he feels entitled to.

## ● *Attitude of Superiority*

The student has a sense of being superior and presents himself as smarter, more creative, more talented, more experienced, and more worldly than others.

## ● *Exaggerated or Pathological Need for Attention*

The student shows an exaggerated, even pathological, need for attention, whether positive or negative, no matter what the circumstances.

● *Externalizes Blame*

The student consistently refuses to take responsibility for his or her own actions and typically faults other people, events or situations for any failings or shortcomings. In placing blame, the student frequently seems impervious to rational argument and common sense.

● *Masks Low Self-esteem*

Though he may display an arrogant, self-glorifying attitude, the student's conduct often appears to veil an underlying low self-esteem. He avoids high visibility or involvement in school activities, and other students may consider him a nonentity.

● *Anger Management Problems*

Rather than expressing anger in appropriate ways and in appropriate circumstances, the student consistently tends to burst out in temper tantrums or melodramatic displays, or to brood in sulky, seething silence. The anger may be noticeably out of proportion to the cause, or may be redirected toward people who had nothing to do with the original incident.

His anger may come in unpredictable and uncontrollable outbursts, and may be accompanied by expressions of unfounded prejudice, dislike, or even hatred toward individuals or groups.

● *Intolerance*

The student often expresses racial or religious prejudice or intolerant attitudes toward minorities, or displays slogans or symbols of intolerance in such things as tattoos, jewelry, clothing, bumper stickers, or book covers.

● *Inappropriate Humor*

The student's humor is consistently inappropriate. Jokes or humorous comments tend to be macabre, insulting, belittling, or mean.

● *Seeks to Manipulate Others*

The student consistently attempts to con and manipulate others and win their trust so they will rationalize any signs of aberrant or threatening behavior.

● *Lack of Trust*

The student is untrusting and chronically suspicious of others' motives and intentions. This lack of trust may approach a clinically paranoid state. He may express the belief that society has no trustworthy institution or mechanism for achieving justice or resolving conflict, and that if something bothers him, he has to settle it in his own way.

## ● *Closed Social Group*

The student appears introverted, with acquaintances rather than friends, or associates only with a single small group that seems to exclude everyone else. Students who threaten or carry out violent acts are not necessarily loners in the classic sense, and the composition and qualities of peer groups can be important pieces of information in assessing the danger that a threat will be acted on.

## ● *Change of Behavior*

The student's behavior changes dramatically. His academic performance may decline, or he may show a reckless disregard for school rules, schedules, dress codes, and other regulations.

## ● *Rigid and Opinionated*

The student appears rigid, judgmental and cynical, and voices strong opinions on subjects about which he or she has little knowledge. He disregards facts, logic, and reasoning that might challenge these opinions.

## ● *Unusual Interest in Sensational Violence*

The student demonstrates an unusual interest in school shootings and other heavily publicized acts of violence. He may declare his admiration for those who committed the acts, or may criticize them for "incompetence" or failing to kill enough people. He may explicitly express a desire to carry out a similar act in his own school, possibly as an act of "justice."

## ● *Fascination with Violence-Filled Entertainment*

The student demonstrates an unusual fascination with movies, TV shows, computer games, music videos or printed material that focus intensively on themes of violence, hatred, control, power, death, and destruction. He may incessantly watch one movie or read and reread one book with violent content, perhaps involving school violence. Themes of hatred, violence, weapons, and mass destruction recur in virtually all his activities, hobbies, and pastimes.

The student spends inordinate amounts of time playing video games with violent themes, and seems more interested in the violent images than in the game itself.

On the Internet, the student regularly searches for web sites involving violence, weapons, and other disturbing subjects. There is evidence the student has downloaded and kept material from these sites.

## ● *Negative Role Models*

The student may be drawn to negative, inappropriate role models such as Hitler, Satan, or others associated with violence and destruction.

### ● *Behavior Appears Relevant to Carrying Out a Threat*

The student appears to be increasingly occupied in activities that could be related to carrying out a threat -- for example, spending unusual amounts of time practicing with firearms or on various violent websites. The time spent in these activities has noticeably begun to exclude normal everyday pursuits such as homework, attending classes, going to work, and spending time with friends.

## *Prong Two: Family Dynamics*

### ● *Turbulent Parent-Child Relationship*

The student's relationship with his parents is particularly difficult or turbulent. This difficulty or turbulence can be uniquely evident following a variety of factors, including recent or multiple moves, loss of a parent, addition of a step parent, etc. He expresses contempt for his parents and dismisses or rejects their role in his life. There is evidence of violence occurring within the student's home.

### ● *Acceptance of Pathological Behavior*

Parents do not react to behavior that most parents would find very disturbing or abnormal. They appear unable to recognize or acknowledge problems in their children and respond quite defensively to any real or perceived criticism of their child. If contacted by school officials or staff about the child's troubling behavior, the parents appear unconcerned, minimize the problem, or reject the reports altogether even if the child's misconduct is obvious and significant.

### ● *Access to Weapons*

The family keeps guns or other weapons or explosive materials in the home, accessible to the student. More important, weapons are treated carelessly, without normal safety precautions; for example, guns are not locked away and are left loaded. Parents or a significant role model may handle weapons casually or recklessly and in doing so may convey to children that a weapon can be a useful and normal means of intimidating someone else or settling a dispute.

### ● *Lack of Intimacy*

The family appears to lack intimacy and closeness. The family has moved frequently and/or recently.

### ● *Student "Rules the Roost"*

The parents set few or no limits on the child's conduct, and regularly give in to his demands.  The student insists on an inordinate degree of privacy, and parents have little information about his activities, school life, friends, or other relationships.

The parents seem intimidated by their child.  They may fear he will attack them physically if they confront or frustrate him, or they may be unwilling to face an emotional outburst, or they may be afraid that upsetting the child will spark an emotional crisis.  Traditional family roles are reversed: for example, the child acts as if he were the authority figure, while parents act as if they were the children.

### ● *No Limits or Monitoring of TV and Internet*

Parents do not supervise, limit or monitor the student's television watching or his use of the Internet.  The student may have a TV in his own room or is otherwise free without any limits to spend as much time as he likes watching violent or otherwise inappropriate shows.  The student spends a great deal of time watching television rather than in activities with family or friends.

Similarly, parents do not monitor computer use or Internet access.  The student may know much more about computers than the parents do, and the computer may be considered off limits to the parents while the student is secretive about his computer use, which may involve violent games or Internet research on violence, weapons, or other disturbing subjects.

### *Prong Three: School Dynamics* *

*\*If an act of violence occurs at a school, the school becomes the scene of the crime. As in any violent crime, it is necessary to understand what it is about the school which might have influenced the student's decision to offend there rather than someplace else.  While it may be difficult for educators/assessors to "critique" or evaluate their own school, one must have some degree of awareness of these unique dynamics - prior to a threat - in order to assess a student's role in the school culture and to develop a better understanding - <u>from the student's perspective</u> - of why he would target his own school.*

### ● *Student's Attachment to School*

Student appears to be "detached" from school, including other students, teachers, and school activities.

### ● *Tolerance for Disrespectful Behavior*

The school does little to prevent or punish disrespectful behavior between individual students or groups of students.  Bullying is part of the school culture and school authorities seem oblivious to it, seldom or never intervening or doing so only selectively. Students frequently act in the roles of bully, victim, or bystander (sometimes, the same student plays different roles in different circumstances). The school atmosphere promotes racial or class divisions or allows them to remain unchallenged.

### ● *Inequitable Discipline*

The use of discipline is inequitably applied - or has the perception of being inequitably applied by students and/or staff.

### ● *Inflexible Culture*

The school's culture -- official and unofficial patterns of behavior, values, and relationships among students, teachers, staff, and administrators -- is static, unyielding, and insensitive to changes in society and the changing needs of newer students and staff.

### ● *Pecking Order Among Students*

Certain groups of students are officially or unofficially given more prestige and respect than others. Both school officials and the student body treat those in the high-prestige groups as though they are more important or more valuable to the school than other students.

### ● *Code of Silence*

A "code of silence" prevails among students. Few feel they can safely tell teachers or administrators if they are concerned about another student's behavior or attitudes. Little trust exists between students and staff.

### ● *Unsupervised Computer Access*

Access to computers and the Internet is unsupervised and unmonitored. Students are able to use the school's computers to play violent computer games or to explore inappropriate web sites such as those that promote violent hate groups or give instructions for bomb-making.

***Schools should maintain documentation of all prior incidents or problems involving students so it can be considered in future threat assessments.***

### *Prong Four: Social Dynamics*

### ● *Media, Entertainment, Technology*

The student has easy and unmonitored access to movies, television shows, computer games, and Internet sites with themes and images of extreme violence.

● *Peer Groups*

The student is intensely and exclusively involved with a group who share a fascination with violence or extremist beliefs. The group excludes others who do not share its interests or ideas. As a result, the student spends little or no time with anyone who thinks differently and is shielded from the "reality check" that might come from hearing other views or perceptions.

● *Drugs and Alcohol*

Knowledge of a student's use of drugs and alcohol and his attitude toward these substances can be important. Any changes in his behavior involving these substances can also be important.

● *Outside Interests*

A student's interests outside of school are important to note, as they can mitigate the school's concern when evaluating a threat or increase the level of concern.

● *The Copycat Effect*

School shootings and other violent incidents that receive intense media attention can generate threats or copycat violence elsewhere. Copycat behavior is very common, in fact. Anecdotal evidence strongly indicates that threats increase in schools nationwide after a shooting has occurred anywhere in the United States. Students, teachers, school administrators and law enforcement officials should be more vigilant in noting disturbing student behavior in the days and weeks or even several months following a heavily publicized incident elsewhere in the country.

# CHAPTER V

## *THE INTERVENTION PROCESS*

A school cannot ignore any threat of violence. Plausible or not, every threat must be taken seriously, investigated, and responded to. A clear, vigorous response is essential for three reasons: first and most important, to make sure that students, teachers, and staff *are* safe (that is, that a threat will not be carried out); second, to assure that they will *feel* safe; and third, to assure that the person making the threat will be supervised and given the treatment that is appropriate and necessary to avoid future danger to others or himself.

It is not the purpose of this paper to recommend any specific forms of intervention for a particular student or type of threat. School disciplinary policies and appropriate treatment approaches should be determined by school administrators and counseling staff, mental health professionals, and other specialists. Rather, the following discussion focuses on two specific issues: (1) the need for schools to adopt a well thought-out system for responding to threats, and (2) guidelines for the role of law enforcement agencies in the threat-response process.

### *Threat Management In Schools*

A clear, consistent, rational, and well-structured system for dealing with threats is vitally important in a school. If students or staff feel that threats are not addressed quickly and sensibly, or if school administrators appear overwhelmed and uncertain at every threat, confidence in the school's ability to maintain a safe environment will be seriously undermined. This in turn can seriously disrupt the school's educational program.

An effective threat management system will include a standardized method for evaluating threats, and consistent policies for responding to them. A standardized approach will help schools construct a data base, with information on the types and frequency of threats, which may help evaluate the effectiveness of school policies. Consistency in threat response can deter future threats if students perceive that any threat will be reported, investigated, and dealt with firmly.

Here are some guidelines for establishing and implementing a threat management system:

***Inform students and parents of school policies:*** A school should publicize its threat response and intervention program at the beginning of every school year (or to new students when they transfer into the school). The school should clearly explain what is expected of students -- for example, students who know about a threat are expected to inform school authorities. The school should also make clear to parents that if their child makes a threat of any kind, they will be contacted and will be expected to provide information to help evaluate the threat.

***Designate a threat assessment coordinator:*** One person in a school -- or perhaps several in a large school -- should be assigned to oversee and coordinate the school's response to all threats. The designated coordinator may be the principal, another administrator, a school psychologist, resource officer, or any other staff member. The school should find appropriate threat assessment training programs for whoever is designated.

When any threat is made, whoever receives it or first becomes aware of it should refer it immediately to the designated coordinator, and school policy should explicitly give the coordinator the necessary authority to make or assist in making quick decisions on how to respond -- including implementing the school's emergency response plan, if the threat warrants.

The coordinator's specific responsibilities will be determined in each school, in accord with the professional judgment of the principal and administrative staff. They could include: arranging for an initial assessment when a threat is received to determine the level of threat; conducting or overseeing an evaluation after the threatener is identified, using the Four-Pronged Assessment Model; developing and refining the threat management system; monitoring intervention in previous cases; establishing liaison with other school staff and outside experts; and maintaining consistency and continuity in the school's threat response procedures.

***Consider forming a Multidisciplinary Team:*** As well as appointing a threat assessment coordinator, schools may decide to establish a multi disciplinary team as another component of the threat assessment system. Schools could draw team members from school staff and other professionals, including trained mental health professionals. The team would constitute an experienced, knowledgeable group that could review threats, consult with outside experts, and provide recommendations and advice to the coordinator and to the school administration. ***It is strongly recommended that a law enforcement representative should either be included as a member of the team or regularly consulted as a resource person.*** Making threats can be a criminal offense, depending on the threat and the laws of each state. Although most school threats may not lead to prosecution, school officials need informed, professional advice on when a criminal violation has occurred and what actions may be required by state or local laws.

**It is especially important that a school not deal with threats by simply kicking the problem out the door. Expelling or suspending a student for making a threat must not be a substitute for careful threat assessment and a considered, consistent policy of intervention. Disciplinary action alone, unaccompanied by any effort to evaluate the threat or the student's intent, may actually exacerbate the danger-- for example, if a student feels unfairly or arbitrarily treated and becomes even angrier and more bent on carrying out a violent act.**

## *The Role of Law Enforcement*

In the vast majority of cases, the decision on whether to involve law enforcement will hinge on the seriousness of the threat: low, medium, or high, under the criteria outlined earlier in this paper.

**Low Level:** A threat that has been evaluated as low level poses little threat to public safety and in most cases would not necessitate law enforcement investigation for a possible criminal offense. (However, law enforcement agencies may be asked for information in connection with a threat of any level.)

Appropriate intervention in a low level case would involve, at a minimum, interviews with the student and his or her parents. If the threat was aimed at a specific person, that person should also be asked about his or her relationship with the threatener and the circumstances that led up to the threat. The response -- disciplinary action and any decision to refer a student for counseling or other form of intervention -- should be determined according to school policies and the judgment of the responsible school administrators.

**Medium Level:** When a threat is rated as medium level, the response should in most cases include contacting law enforcement agencies, as well as other sources, to obtain additional information (and possibly reclassify the threat into the high or low category).

A medium-level threat will sometimes, though not necessarily, warrant investigation as a possible criminal offense.

**High Level:** Almost always, if a threat is evaluated as high level, the school should immediately inform the appropriate law enforcement agency. A response plan, which should have been designed ahead of time and rehearsed by both school and law enforcement personnel, should be implemented, and law enforcement should be informed and involved in whatever subsequent actions are taken in response to threat.

A high-level threat is highly likely to result in criminal prosecution.

## *Examples of Threats*

**Example #1: Low-Level Threat:** *Student John Jones sends another student an e-mail message saying: "You are a dead man."*

### *Step One -- Referral*

The parents and student who received the message bring the message to the attention of the school's Threat Assessment Coordinator the following morning.

_Step Two -- Threat Assessment - Based on the following reasons the e-mail threat is
assessed as a low level of threat_

(1) Threat is vague and indirect: "You are a dead man."

(2) Threat lacks detail. There is no specific information on how the threat is to be carried
out, on the motive or intent, or on the time and place where the threat is to be acted on.

(3) The means to carry out the threat is unknown.

_Step Three -- Four-Pronged Assessment_

(1) Since the threatener's identity is known, background information can be obtained from
faculty members who knew the student and his family before the threat was made. They picture
him as somewhat immature and prone to losing his temper, but report no seriously troubling traits
or changes in behavior.

(2) Interviews with the student and his parents establish that he has no access to weapons.
No other information emerges to indicate that the student has made any actual preparations or
seriously intends to carry out the threat.

(3) The target of the threat is interviewed. His responses also suggest the threat is
unlikely to be acted on: "We've had arguments before; he gets mad and says stupid things but he
gets over it."

_Step Four -- Evaluation and Response_

Based on the evaluation of the threat and the four-pronged assessment of the student, the
**OVERALL** assessment is that this is a low level threat. A law enforcement contact or resource
person is advised of the incident, but administrative action will be determined by school
authorities in accordance with school policy.


**Example #2: Medium-Level Threat:** Tom Murphy, a ninth-grader, makes a videotape
for one of his classes. The tape shows student actors shooting at other students on the school
grounds, using long-barreled guns that appear real. On the videotape, the actor-students are
heard yelling at other students, laughing, and making off-color remarks, while aiming their
weapons at others. Murphy's teacher receives the tape and becomes concerned.

_Step One -- Referral_

The teacher brings the tape to the Threat Assessment Coordinator, who in turn calls a
meeting of the available members of the school's Multidisciplinary Team.

*Step Two -- Threat Assessment - Based on the following, the videotape is determined to be a medium level of threat until more information can be obtained.*

(1) The threat is specific. Murphy and fellow students who are posing as shooters, are pointing weapons at other students pretending to be victims. *However*, it is unknown if Murphy and his friends actually intended to carry out the threat, and if the weapons displayed in the videotape are real. Some of the comments heard on the tape are explicitly threatening but all of the students are laughing and it is therefore unclear whether they are speaking seriously or joking.

(2) The guns used in the videotape may or may not be real.

(3) The "script" used in the videotape suggests that the threateners have given some thought to how the threat will be carried out regarding place and time.

(4) It is unclear if the videotape, with all of its detail, is a serious prelude to real threat, or a joke.

*Step Three -- Four-Pronged Assessment*

(1) The Threat Assessment Coordinator and members of the Multidisciplinary Team gather additional background on each of the students who appear in the videotape. Information is sought from faculty members who knew the students and their families prior to the incident.

(2) Students and parents are interviewed and it is determined that the guns used in the videotape were toys, and the students have no access to real weapons. No other information is provided that would elevate the level of the threat.

*Step Four -- Evaluation and Response*

Based on evaluation of the videotape and the assessment of the ninth-grader who organized the filming, this is reclassified as a low level threat. Law enforcement officers conducted the investigation, but administrative action is left to the discretion of the school.

**Example #3: High-Level Threat:** A high school principal receives an anonymous phone call at 7:30 a.m. The caller says: "There is a pipe bomb scheduled to go off in the gym at noon today. I placed the bomb in the locker of one of the seniors. Don't worry, it's not my locker. I just placed it there because I can see it from where I will be sitting -- and will know if someone goes to check on it."

*Step One -- Immediate Law Enforcement Involvement and Emergency Response*

The principal calls a designated contact in the local police department as provided in the school's emergency response plan. The emergency plan is put into effect.

*Step Two -- Threat Assessment - Based on the following, this anonymous threat was determined to be a high level of threat.*

(1) The threat is direct and specific. The caller identifies a specific weapon he will use as well as a location for the assault, and the time the threat will be carried out.

(2) The content of the threat suggests the caller has taken concrete steps to carry out the threat, i.e., he has placed the locker under surveillance in order to determine if someone checks on it.

(3) The identity of the threatener is unknown. His means, knowledge, and resources to construct a pipe bomb are unknown.

*Step Three -- Because the threatener is unidentified, the Four-Pronged Assessment cannot be conducted.*

*Step Four -- Evaluation and Response*

Because of its specific detail and plausible nature, this is determined to be a high level threat posing a serious danger to students and staff and requiring immediate intervention by law enforcement. If the threatener is subsequently identified, he is likely to be charged with a criminal offense and prosecuted.

# CHAPTER VI

## *RECOMMENDATIONS AND CONCLUSIONS*

As has been noted, the threat assessment and intervention model presented in this paper was a focus of discussion at the l999 NCAVC Symposium in Leesburg, Virginia. Noting that additional research can further develop and refine the concepts and methods embraced in this model, the symposium made the following recommendation:

*There is a compelling need to field test, evaluate and further develop these threat assessment recommendations and to develop appropriate interventions designed to respond to the mental health needs of the students involved. This is a pressing public health need which could be addressed through multidisciplinary collaboration by educators, mental health professionals and law enforcement.*

The symposium also recommended that additional research should include studies on the following topics:

- The presence of psychopathic and narcissistic personality traits in offenders convicted of charges arising from a school shooting.

- The significance and relevance of verbal and written "leakage" for threat assessment and predicting future violence.

- Determining which specific school dynamics appear to be significant risk factors in schools.

- The influence and relevance of suicide and suicide ideation in adolescents who have become involved in school shootings.

- Identifying significant commonalities between the school shooter's personality, background, and family circumstances, and those of other violent adolescents.

- Identifying significant commonalities and differences between the adolescent school shooter and adult offenders involved in workplace violence.

- A review of relevant state and federal laws and confidentiality requirements that prevent or impede sharing information that can help educators, law enforcement and social service agencies evaluate a student to assess intent, means, and motivation and the risk of his carrying out a threatened violent act.

The symposium made these additional recommendations:

31

*Investigating school violence:* To further develop a basis for assessment, after a school shooting or other act of school violence, investigations should be designed to obtain more information in the four areas of the student's life: (1) personality, (2) family dynamics, (3) school dynamics, and (4) social dynamics.

*Training:* To make effective use of the assessment and intervention procedures outlined in this monograph, school administrators and staff members should receive additional training in the fundamentals of the threat assessment, adolescent development and violence, and other mental health issues relevant to the area of adolescent development  Specialized training is needed for those assigned to conduct or supervise the assessment process.

Training is also needed to educate and sensitize students about "leakage" and its significance in dealing with the threat of violence.  Students are often in the best position to see and hear signs or cues of potential violence, and training should stress that ignoring those cues or remaining silent can be dangerous for themselves as well as others.  Training should also confront the common teenage "code of silence" and students' reluctance to be branded as a "snitch" or to violate a friend's confidence.

Other suggestions relating to training include:

- Establish "Internal Teams" in schools to find ways to encourage students to come forward in a confidential manner with information about threatening behavior.

- Encourage "Student Assistance Programs" in which concerned teachers would come together and discuss students who are having academic problems, behavioral problems, or problems at home.

- Establish "Peer Assistance Groups" that will encourage students to come forward with information about possible threatening behavior in other students, and provide support to overcome self-doubts or guilty feelings about breaking the "code of silence."

- Develop programs to help parents recognize when their child may be in emotional trouble or socially isolated or rejected, and help parents become more knowledgeable about where to get help and more willing to seek it.

Questions of how threat assessment training should be set up or how it should be funded are beyond the scope of this monograph.  Representatives of national educational organizations and experts identified on page 45 of this monograph that participated in the Leesburg Symposium indicated interest in exploring these issues in concert with local, state and federal law enforcement.


## CONCLUSIONS

Violence -- whether in a school, home, workplace, or on the street -- is a complex issue with complex causes and consequences. Imagining that there are easy answers and instant solutions is counterproductive: there is no easy way to attack the causes and no simple formula that can predict who will commit a violent act. It is also true, however, that violent behavior develops progressively, that making a threat represents a stage in an evolutionary process, and that there are observable signs along the way that most of us can see if we know what to look for.

Overall, the level of violence in American schools is falling, not rising. But the shock and fear generated by the recent succession of school shootings and other violent acts in schools -- and by violence in society at large -- have led to intense public concern about the danger of school violence. In this atmosphere, it is critically important for schools to respond to all threats swiftly, responsibly, fairly, and sensitively, and with an understanding that all threats are not equal.

It is not enough to react only to the threatening message, whether spoken, written, or symbolic. It is also vital to assess whether the person who made the threat has the intent, means, and motivation to carry it out. The procedure presented in this monograph can help schools assess a threat and the threatener, evaluate the risk, and respond appropriately and effectively.

We know that students will continue to make threats in schools, and that most will never carry them out. The use of this assessment/intervention model will help school authorities identify and deal with the high-risk threats that are the major concern, and respond to less serious threats in a measured way. The same distinction needs to be recognized in the larger world outside the school as well, for the same reasons. Threats in schools are not just the schools' problem; therefore, neither is the solution.

# APPENDIX A

The threat assessment model recommended in this monograph was developed in part from NCAVC's analysis of eighteen school-shooting cases around the country. Analysts also drew on material from other cases in which NCAVC prepared threat assessments in response to a threatened act of school violence. NCAVC's findings were used to formulate questions and topics for discussion at the July 1999 Leesburg symposium on school shooting.

The methodology for collecting and considering data from the eighteen cases is summarized below. Following that is a brief explanation of how the material was presented and considered at the symposium.

## *Methodology*

*Identification of cases:* Eighteen schools throughout the country were included in this study. Actual shootings occurred at fourteen of the schools. In the other four, the student or students involved planned a shooting and made significant preparations, but were detected and preempted by law enforcement, and arrests were made before a shooting took place.

Five of the schools were middle schools and thirteen were high schools. All but one were public schools. The cases involved single and multiple offenders. Criminal and/or civil litigation was pending in all but one of the cases.

In addition to these eighteen cases, current NCAVC cases were also included in this study. These were cases in which a threat assessment was being prepared by the NCAVC.

*Acquisition of case materials:* School and law enforcement officials involved in each of the incidents were contacted and told about the NCAVC study and the scheduled symposium.

NCAVC requested information on each case specifically relevant to the area of threat assessment. The material included:

- A summary of the incident, as described in investigation reports.

- Tapes or transcripts of interviews with the offender(s).

- Witness statements.

- Interviews with persons who knew the students and families and provided information about offenders' background.
- Crime scene photographs and videos.

- Counseling and psychiatric reports and evaluations.

- Examples of the shooter's writings, drawings, doodles, essays, letters, poems, songs, videotapes, and audiotapes.

- School records and any class work that would provide insight into the shooter and his relationships with teachers and other students.

- Pre-sentence psychiatric reports and psychiatric evaluations by either defense or prosecution experts.

- Other pertinent case materials.

In addition to reviewing case materials, NCAVC agents interviewed law enforcement and school personnel who were familiar with each case to obtain additional insight about the shooters, their families and background, the social climate and atmosphere of the school, and any other factors or stressors which may have affected the student before or at the time of the shooting.

*Case review:* Case materials were reviewed by NCAVC agents with extensive experience in the area of threat assessment. After examining the available information about the shooter, his behavior before and after the shooting, how victims were selected, and events at the scene, the analysts sought to identify and describe critical aspects, including:

- The shooter's behavior patterns in relating to family members, peers, teachers, and persons in authority.

- Disciplinary problems noted or reported by school staff or parents.

- Reported incidents of aggressive behavior and/or anger management problems.

- Type, style and content of the student's writing and artwork, including journals, poems, essays, drawings, doodles, and videotapes.

- Student's preferences in literature, artwork and Internet sites.

- Student's circle of friends, including girlfriends, and his apparent role in that group.

- Changes in the student's behavior that were noted by others prior to the incident.

- Statements by the student directly or indirectly telling others ahead of time about a planned shooting.

- Extent of planning and preparations before the crime.

- Student's behavior on the day of the shooting.

- Types of weapons brought to the scene.

- Type and extent of the interaction between the shooter and victims before and during the shooting.

- Student's behavior after the shooting.

- Results of prosecution.

### *Use of Case Reviews at the Symposium*

Data from these case reviews was used at the Leesburg symposium in three ways: (1) as focus for the expert panels to stimulate further questions and answers; (2) as material for discussion in the breakout groups; and (3) to augment findings of the breakout groups.

The *expert panel* portion of the symposium program consisted of four three-hour sessions. Panelists were specialists in the fields of adolescent development, adolescent violence, mental health, school dynamics and school violence. At each session, panelists presented current research findings and offered ideas on how recent research in their areas of expertise may bear on issues of school violence, school shootings and threat assessment.

In addition to the expert panels, two-hour School Incident Panels were held on four specific school shootings. At each of these sessions, teachers, administrators, and investigators involved in the particular case presented information on the incident, the shooter and his background, the dynamics of the school, and the course and outcome of criminal prosecution.

*Breakout groups* were convened on the fourth day of the symposium. Each group had approximately fifteen people, including educators, mental health professionals, researchers, and representatives of state, local and federal law enforcement agencies. The breakout groups were assigned the task of identifying behavioral traits and characteristics shown by students then, when considered in their totality, could be indicative of threatening behavior. In addition, the groups were asked to discuss different forms of intervention appropriate to threats with varying levels of seriousness and immediacy.

A member of the NCAVC with training in threat assessment, risk assessment, and personality assessment was assigned to each breakout group as a facilitator, whose role was to lead and focus discussions. The breakout sessions were not tape recorded, in order to protect confidential information, but each group appointed a recorder to keep a written record of the ideas discussed.

Conclusions from the breakout discussions were presented on the final day of the symposium.

# APPENDIX B

## *Suggested Readings*

Benedek, E.P., & Cornell, D.G. (Eds.). (1989). *Juvenile homicide.* Washington, DC: American Psychiatric Press.

Berman, A.L., & Jobes, D.A. (1991). *Adolescent suicide: Assessment and intervention.* Washington, DC: American Psychological Association.

Bushman, B.J., & Baumeister, R.F. (1998). Threatened egotism, narcissism, self-esteem, and direct and displaced aggression: Does self-love or self-hate lead to violence? *Journal of Personality and Social Psychology, 75* (1), 219-229.

Centerwall, B.S. (1992). Television and violence: The scale of the problem and where to go from here. *The Journal of the American Medical Association, 267* (22), 3059-3060.

Cornell, D.G., & Sheras, P.L. (1998). Common errors in school crisis response: Learning from our mistakes. *Psychology in the Schools, 35* (3), 297-307.

Cornell, D.G., Miller, C., & Benedek, E.P. (1988). MMPI profiles of adolescents charged with homicide. *Behavioral Sciences & the Law, 6* (3), 401-407.

Cornell, D.G. (1990). Prior adjustment of violent juvenile offenders. *Law and Human Behavior, 14* (6),  569-577.

Dietz, P.E., Matthews, D.P., & Van Duyne, C. (1991). Threatening and otherwise inappropriate letters to Hollywood celebrities. *Journal of Forensic Sciences, 36*, 185-209.

Dietz, P.E. (1986). Mass, serial and sensational homicides. *Bulletin New York Academy of Medicine, 62* (5), 477-491.

Dwyer, K.P., Osher, D., & Warger, C. (1998). *Early warning, timely response:  A guide to safe schools.* Washington, DC: U.S. Department of Education (DOE) and Department of Justice (DOJ).

Dwyer, K.P., & Osher, D. (2000). *Safeguarding our children: An action guide.* Washington DC: U.S. Department of Education (DOE) and Department of Justice (DOJ).

Frick, P.J., & Christian, R.E. (1999). Age trends in association between parenting practices and conduct problems. *Behavior Modification, 23* (1), 106-128.

Frick, P.J. (1995). Callous-unemotional traits and conduct problems: A two-factor model of psychopathy in children. *Issues in Criminological and Legal Psychology, 24*, 47-51.

Garbarino, J. (1999). *Lost boys: Why our sons turn violent and how we can save them.* New York: Free Press.

Garbarino, J. (1995). *Raising children in a socially toxic environment.* San Francisco: Jossey-Bass.

Group for the Advancement of Psychiatry. (1996). *Adolescent suicide.* Washington, DC: American Psychiatric Press.

Hardwick, P.J., & Rowton-Lee, M.A. (1996). Adolescent homicide: Towards assessment of risk. *Journal of Adolescence, 19*, 263-276.

Hare, R.D. (1998). Psychopathy, affect and behavior. In D. J. Cooke, A.E. Forth, & R.D. Hare (Eds.), *Psychopathy: Theory, research and implications for society* (pp. 105-137). Dordrecht, Netherlands: Kluwer Academic Publishers.

Hare, R.D. (1993). *Without conscience: The disturbing world of the psychopaths among us.* New York: Pocket Books.

Hart, S.D., & Hare, R.D. (1997). Psychopathy: Assessment and association with criminal conduct. In D. M. Stoff, J. Brieling, & J. Maser (Eds.), *Handbook of antisocial behavior* (pp. 22-35). New York: John Wiley.

Kernberg, O.F. (1993). The psychopathology of hatred. *In Rage, power and aggression.* (pp. 61-79). New Haven: Yale University Press.

Lynam, D.R. (1998). Early identification of the fledgling psychopath: Locating the psychopathic child in the current nomenclature. *Journal of Abnormal Psychology, 107* (4), 566-575.

Malmquist, C.P. (1996). *Homicide: A psychiatric perspective.* Washington, DC: American Psychiatric Press.

Malmquist, C.P. (1980). Psychiatric aspects of familicide. *Bulletin American Academy of Psychiatry and Law,* 8, 298-304.

Maris, R.W., Berman, A.L., Maltsberger, J.T., & Yufit, R.I. (Eds.). (1992). *Assessment and prediction of suicide.* New York: Guilford.

Meloy, J.R. (1997). Predatory violence during mass murder. *Journal of Forensic Sciences, 42* (2), 326-329.

Miller, D., & Looney, J. (1974). The prediction of adolescent homicide: Episodic dyscontrol and dehumanization. *The American Journal of Psychoanalysis, 34,* 187-198.

Monahan, J., & Steadman, H. J. (Eds.). (1994). *Violence and mental disorder: Developments in risk assessment.* Chicago: The University of Chicago Press.

Nichols, K.S. (in press) Differential emotional expression of children while viewing violent movie scenes. *Clinical Psychology, Science and Practice.*

Nichols, K.S. (1999, November). Children need help interpreting TV violence. *Lawrence Journal World, 1D-2D.*

Ochberg, F. M. (1996). The counting method for ameliorating traumatic memories. *Journal of Traumatic Stress,* 9 (4), 873-880.

Ochberg, F. M. (Ed.). (1988). *Post-traumatic therapy and victims of violence.* New York: Brunner/Mazzel

Palermo, G.B., & Ross, L.E. (1999). Mass murder, suicide, and moral development: Can we separate the adults from the juveniles? *International Journal of Offender Therapy and Comparative Criminology,* 43 (1), 8-20.

Palermo, G.B. (1995). Adolescent criminal behavior: Is TV violence one of the culprits? *International Journal of Offender Therapy and Comparative Criminology,* 39, 11-22.

Stack, S. (1997). Homicide followed by suicide: An analysis of Chicago data. *Criminology, 35* (3), 435-445.

Twemlow, S.W., Sacco, F.C., & Williams, P. (1996, Summer). A clinical and interactionist perspective on the bully-victim-bystander relationship. *Bulletin of the Menninger Clinic,* 60 (3), 296-313.

Twemlow, S.W., & Sacco, F.C. (1998). A multi-level conceptual framework for understanding the violent community. In H. V. Hall & L. C. Whitaker (Eds.), *Collective violence effective strategies for assessing and interviewing in fatal group and institution alaggression* (pp. 575-599). New York: CRC Press.

# APPENDIX C

## *Proposals*

The following proposals, offered by persons attending the 1999 Leesburg Symposium, list possible actions that can be taken in a school to strengthen its threat response program. These are not recommendations of the FBI.

- Produce public service announcements for the community encouraging students to come forward with information about "leakage" or other disturbing behavior, and presenting those who do so in a positive light.

- Establish an Emergency Response Plan in coordination with law enforcement agencies, mental health and emergency medical services, and other schools in the district. This plan should include a system for notifying police and other emergency response agencies. All staff should be familiar with the notification procedure.

- Consider preparing a Memorandum of Understanding between schools, law enforcement agencies and other agencies outlining responsibilities and actions to be taken in the event of some type of incident.

- Establish an internal distress code system within the school for teachers and other staff.

- Prepare a Crisis Negotiation Plan and an Investigative Response Plan, in concert with appropriate agencies. (These plans may be included in a memorandum of understanding.)

- Establish a program aimed at students and parents that will seek to encourage the reporting of threats, problem behavior and "leakage." Such a program should include distributing a list of contacts, phone numbers, and if applicable, the hours when each contact person will be available.

- Start a "lunch buddy program" in which concerned adults come to the school on a regular basis to interact with students.

- Seek financial support from the corporate sector in the community that will help maintain mental health services in the schools, summer programs, and "adopt-a-school" programs.

- Provide training to help parents track their child's use of the internet, and raise awareness of the disturbing effect extensive viewing of violent videos can have on some children.

- Foster good relations with law enforcement and community mental health agencies through mutual training classes, and presentations for staff.

- Establish school resource officer positions in schools.

- Establish or strengthen parent volunteer programs in the schools.

- Provide training for students on relevant subjects such as interpersonal communication, conflict resolution, anger management, coping with depression, family tensions, and identifying and reporting threatening behavior.

- Make use of student peer groups in the intervention program.

- Seek volunteer mentors from the community as one means of helping students who have been identified as requiring intervention.

# APPENDIX D

## Acknowledgments

## Major Contributors

Larry G. Ankrom
Supervisory Special Agent
NCAVC
FBI Academy
Quantico, Virginia 22135
(703) 632-4257

Marie L. Dyson
Supervisory Special Agent
NCAVC
FBI Academy
Quantico, Virginia 22135
(703) 632-4338

Kelly A. McEniry
Supervisory Special Agent/Chief
  Division Counsel
CIRG
FBI Academy
Quantico, Virginia 22135
(703 632-4400

Gregory B. Saathoff, M.D.
Associate Professor of Clinical
Psychiatry - University of Virginia
gbs3@virginia.edu

## Editor

Arnold R. Isaacs

# Contributing Experts

| | |
|---|---|
| Dr. Lanny Berman<br>Suicidology<br>(202) 237-2280<br>berm101@ix.netcom.com | Carl Malmquist, M.D., M.S.<br>Homicidal Violence<br>(612) 926-8180<br>malq001@atlas.socsci.umn.edu |
| Dr. Dewey Cornell<br>Clinical and Forensic Psychology<br>University of Virginia<br>(804) 924-0793<br>dcornell@virginia.edu | Kathie Nichols, Ph.D.<br>Clinical Psychologist<br>(785) 350-5399 |
| Park Dietz, M.D., Ph.D.<br>President, Threat Assessment Group<br>School Violence Prevention Training and<br>Consultation<br>(949) 644-3537<br>tagexpert@aol.com | Frank M. Ochberg, M.D.<br>Post-Traumatic Stress, Psychiatry, Journalism &<br>Criminal Justice<br>Critical Incident Response<br>(517) 349-6333<br>ochberg@earthlink.net |
| Kevin P. Dwyer<br>Past President<br>National Association of School Psychologists<br>(301) 657-0270<br>kdwyer@naspweb.org | David Osher, Ph.D.<br>Director, Center for Effective Collaboration &<br>Practice<br>American Institute's for Research<br>(202) 944-5373<br>dosher@air.org |
| Philip Erdberg, Ph.D.<br>Clinical Psychology and Personality Assessment | Gregory Saathoff, M.D.<br>Associate Professor of Clinical Psychiatry<br>University of Virginia<br>gbs3a@virginia.edu |
| James Garbarino, Ph.D.<br>Professor of Human Development<br>Cornell University<br>(607) 255-4704 | Frank Sacco, Ph.D.<br>Child and Family Mental Health<br>(413) 739-5572<br>FCSacco@aol.com |
| Robert D. Hare, Ph.D.<br>Forensic Psychology, Psychopathy, & Risk of<br>Violence<br>(604) 822-3611<br>rhare@interchange.ubc.ca<br>www.hare.org | Stuart W. Twemlow, M.D.<br>Psychiatry and Psychoanalysis<br>(785) 272-5222 |
| | Tim White, Ph.D.<br>Journalist and Media Consultant<br>(703) 524-0844 or (216) 344-7434<br>Twhitecom@aol.com |

# NCAVC Contributors

Kristen R. Beyer

Alan C. Brantley

Tina S. Breede

Diana Cacciola

James T. Clemente

Charles K. Dorsey

Janice M. Dylewski

Stephen E. Etter

W. Hagmaier III

Pamela J. Hairfield

Timothy G. Huff

Wayne R. Koka

Christopher Lawlor

Cynthia J. Lent

Dreama S. Long

Wayne D. Lord

Pamela O. Merryman

U.K. Miller

Roger A. Montgomery

Robert J. Morton

Thomas M. Neer

Eugene A. Rugala

Mark Safarik

Joy Lynn E. Shelton

Rebecca A. Tovar

Ronald F. Tunkel

## Other Contributors

| | |
|---|---|
| Colette Lee Corcoran | Gary W. Noesner |
| Edward F. Davis | Sharon M. Pagaling |
| Philip F. Donegan Jr. | Jon D. Perry |
| Steven R. Fiddler | Wayne D. Porter |
| Elizabeth Ford | Dennis McCormick |
| John H. Freiwald | Mike L. Morrow |
| Faye E. Greenlee | Beth Mullarkey |
| G. Dwayne Fuselier | Neil F. Purtell |
| Barbara Haskins | David J. Raymond Jr. |
| John Martin Huber | Terri E. Royster |
| Dan G. Hodges | Mary Claire Smith |
| Nancy Houston | Gilbert L. Surles, Jr. |
| Roy H. Johnson | Melissa L. Thomas |
| Brian Kiernan | Jim A. Van Allen |
| Ann Kirkland-Nickel | Kelly Wade |
| John C. Lanata | Ronald P. Walker |
| John G. Lang Jr. | Glenn L. Woods |
| Carl D. Malloy | James Zopp |

*The FBI wishes to thank all of the men and women who participated in the July 1999 Leesburg, Virginia Symposium. Their experiences, insights and contributions were invaluable and contributed significantly to the development of this monograph. Due to confidentiality issues, we are not able to list each of these participants individually.*